Going Through Home Again
A Memoir

Lonnie Gable Jr.

Going Through Home Again

Acknowledgments

I would like to gratefully dedicate this book to Pastor J.C. Thompson, and the congregation of the Tarrant City Church of God, in Alabama. There are so many individuals to name that were instrumental in my coming to know Jesus as Lord. First, I would like to recognize Rex Taylor, the first person to invite me to attend a revival at Tarrant City. I also thank Wayne Chambers, Caroline Oliver, Tom and Gladys Walton, Katherine Walton, Patsy Crain, Herman (Hank) Thompson, Earl Thompson, and the evangelist Billy Franklin. This is a beginning list of precious people that were instrumental in my salvation experience and I am eternally grateful.

I grew up in a home without a knowledge, or understanding of God. Alcohol and physical abuse was the norm, making me unaware that there was any other way of the world. My mother was a professing Methodist, but she was sick most of the time I was growing up, and passed away when I was eight. The only time I remember being in church with her was at her funeral. When I first walked into the Tarrant City church, it was as if I had entered another reality. There were people shouting, falling out, and speaking in other tongues. I did not understand what was happening at the time, and I was really frightened. However, I returned the second night of service and God took a hold of my heart.

Going Through Home Again

I would like to also dedicate this book to my wife, Patricia Gable. She has been the source of strength and encouragement throughout my life. She has always truly lived a Christian lifestyle. She has been a blessing, as the mother of our three children, Teresa, Gary, and Michael. All of our children have been very supportive of my ministry throughout my entire life. I would like to give a special thanks to the Church of God that has allowed me to serve in many wonderful churches, with some wonderful people. Above all, I dedicate this book to the Lord Jesus Christ, who loved me so much, that He died on a cruel cross, so that I could live.

Going through home again is neither a geographical journey, nor is it a mental sojourn. It is a painful, spiritual experience, to come to terms with our past. If we go through home again, some of us will have to forgive, and perhaps put our arms around another, to ask for forgiveness. We may need to sing the doxology, over the undeserving. This work intends to teach the next generation to embrace, bless, and forgive, those who have hurt them.

Editor's Note: Names in this work have been changed to protect the privacy of the individuals, and their families.

Foreword

I remember the first time I met Lonnie Gable at the parsonage of Broadmoor Church of God. I was a local life insurance man in the area and Brother Gable's policy had been transferred to my agency. I introduced myself, and began to size him up in my mind.

I thought he had been to a major university; definitely a theological seminary graduate, with advanced degrees; no doubt. As I got to know Lonnie, I realized his experience and demeanor came from a very prestigious institution. It is known as the *School of Hard Knocks*! This book is a saga outlining a man's rise from meager beginnings to achieve success in a life beyond his imagination. I was privileged to travel with Lonnie to his hometown, and see the area where he lived as a boy. Get ready to laugh, cry, be amazed, be entertained, and above all, be uplifted as you read this story.

God chose Lonnie Gable to live a life of encouragement to others. He has been that encouragement many times, for over twenty-eight years to myself, and my wife, Ginny. He first was our pastor; as we became friends, he became someone the two of us consider family. We know you will be blessed by reading how God found, directed, and led Lonnie Gable from Bug Tussle, Alabama, to the pulpit of some of the largest Church of God congregations.

Mike and Ginny Mason

Going Through Home Again

Table of Contents	Page
Acknowledgements	2
Foreword	4
Chapter 1: Family History	6
Chapter 2: The Beginning	10
Chapter 3: The Call of God	20
Chapter 4: The Preaching Begins	26
Chapter 5: Building the Temple	41
Chapter 6: The Testing of Our Faith	45
Chapter 7: A New Culture & Experience	49
Chapter 8: Big Cities & Bright Lights	58
Chapter 9: The Family is Separated for the First Time	70
Chapter 10: Once More Around the Riverbend	78
Archives	84

1
FAMILY HISTORY

Periodically we need to learn to go through home again.[1] This quote is attributed to Carlyle Marney, and expressed perfectly why I began this project. It took me a long time to understand the significance of that statement, but when it finally sank in, I saw the beauty of it. And that is why I have chosen to borrow those words as the title of this work. Henri Nouwen, a Jesuit Priest, and former Yale professor once said, *There is no hope for the future as long as the past remains unreceived, unconfessed, and unforgiven.*[2] Perhaps that is what motivated me to write this story.

While writing this work, I prayed that God would put His approval upon it, making it a blessing, and a source of encouragement to all who read it. Going through home again has always been recognized as an essential and necessary task. Our nation recognizes that fact. That is why we celebrate Independence Day and Thanksgiving. It is just a way that we all get together as Americans, go through home again, and rediscover the rock from which we were hewn. Institutions, such as the church, go through home again. Every time we celebrate

---

[1] Shurden, Walter B. "Roots and Wings-The Mercer Baptist Tradition." The Center for Baptist Studies, 19 Jan. 2006. Web. 26 May 2014.

[2] Shurden, Walter B. "The Importance of Collecting, Preserving, and Disseminating Baptist History." The Center for Baptist Studies, 31 Mar. 2001. Web. 26 May 2014.

Going Through Home Again

Christmas, the empty tomb; every time we gather around the Lord's Table, and take the Sacrament in hand, we are going through home again, and remembering how we got hold of our faith. Families go through home again, when we gather together, and that special little someone blows out the candles, while others applaud and cheer. We reflect upon how it was when we brought that little bundle of joy home from the hospital in that old beat up Ford, or Chevy car. The neighbors, friends, and relatives gathered in to see the newest addition to the family. There were a lot of comments about how much hair she had, or how fat his little cheeks were. One of the little siblings once said, perhaps with a tinge of jealousy, *Well I think she is ugly.* We are just going through home again, remembering what it was that shaped our lives.

    As I have grown older, I have more pressingly felt the desire to go through home again myself, and my daughter Teresa has pushed me for several years to write my story. I will begin with a little bit of my family background, including my ancestry. The Gabel family came to America in 1738 when Johann Henry Gabel, and his wife Lodusca Oswalt arrived in Philadelphia, Pennsylvania. Johann was an immigrant from Germany, possibly accompanied by his two brothers named Abraham and Anthony. Anthony was said to have also brought his two sons. Johann worked for some time after arriving in America as an indentured servant to Captain Brotherick at Port

Going Through Home Again

Royal, in order to repay his family's cost of sea passage. After fulfilling the terms of this contract, he moved to South Carolina in 1747. Family records show that in 1760 he moved to Georgia, but returned to South Carolina in 1776, where he died in 1812. Johann had a son named Hamon, who had a son named Jakob. Jakob moved to Carroll County, Georgia, where he is buried at the Union Grove church, near a stream called Sweetwater Creek. Jakob's son, William, appears to be the first Gabel to move to Alabama, possibly in the late 1840's, where a census worker changed the spelling of *Gabel* to *Gable*. William is the common link between our family, and the Gable family from Duck River Baptist Church, near Cullman. William's wife is buried at Duck River Cemetery, next to her son Jacob, who was commonly referred to as *Jake*.

Jacob's son, Joseph, was my grandfather. My father was born in 1900, and his name was Lonnie Gable Sr. whom I am named after by accident. My intended name was simply to be LJ. There was a mix up by the attending doctor and my legal name became Lonnie Gable Jr. My family, and eventually my wife always called me LJ. My dad, Lonnie, married Ethel Freeman on July 21st, 1923, where they started their lives together. I think about those times, and wonder if they would have done something different, if they had known what little time they really had.

Going Through Home Again

| *Peggy Sue & Wendell* |

2
THE BEGINNING

Lonnie and Ethel Gable settled in Cullman, Alabama, and began their family that same year. The couple eventually had eight children. I was the sixth child born on August 27th, 1936. I was born in a small frame house, which would soon be demolished, and a mule barn would be erected on the spot. I was the brunt of many jokes. Everyone who knew me would declare that I was born in a mule barn. After giving birth to her fifth child in 1930, the physician advised Lonnie and Ethel that she should never have another baby, or it could kill her.

Three babies were born after they had been advised, Lonnie (LJ), Wendell, and Betty. Two of their children had already died before we were born; Theolene A. Gable, born 1932, died September 1st, 1933; Alvin L. Gable was born in 1934, and died April 30th, 1935. *The hand of destiny is sometimes seemingly cruel to the poor.* I experienced this when my mother Ethel died. I was eight years old, my sister Betty was four, and my brother Wendell was thirteen months. The next year after Mother died, my sister Peggy Sue died. Peggy married a man named Alfford Leroy Lavvorn, when she was fourteen years old. Daddy evidently signed for her to get married. Mr. Lavvorn was twenty-one years of age. This is according to information received from my oldest sister, Onvy (Jane) Jones. Mr. Lavvorn got married again after her death, and was divorced

Going Through Home Again

in 1969, then died in 1974. He is buried in the Corinth cemetery in Joppy, Alabama. Peggy died August 15th, 1946, from a septic abortion, according to her death certificate. We grew up in unimaginable poverty. A part of the problem was because my dad had a drinking problem. Many of my relatives were alcoholics. There was a great deal of physical abuse in the family, even though in those years it may not have been considered abuse. I am sure he dealt with us kids the way his dad had reared him, and his siblings.

    My father was abusive toward my mother, my siblings, and myself. When she passed away the abuse and drinking worsened. I know that our children and grandchildren get tired of hearing these stories, but I really did walk three miles, round trip, (and yes, sometimes in the snow), to the elementary school on the east side of Cullman. One winter, I went barefooted so late into the year that it snowed while I was in school and I walked home barefooted in the snow. That same year, I was walking past the storefronts of downtown Cullman. I stopped at a local shoe store and I peered through the window. The shop owner happened to see me looking and asked, *Son, don't you have any shoes?* I was so embarrassed. I said suddenly, *I have shoes mister! I just don't like wearin' them!* I ran as fast as I could down the block and around a corner. In a little alcove, I cried. I kept asking myself why I lied to the shop owner. If I had told the truth, maybe he would have given me some shoes. When I started

Going Through Home Again

preaching, I would use that story to symbolize people and their pride. Many people are afraid to simply ask God to take care of their needs. They will lie to Him and tell him, they are ok. But he knows, much like that shop owner did with me, that we need help getting through life. By the time I entered the seventh grade, my dad had remarried Lillie Mae Buchanan. Very early in that school year she fixed my normal lunch for school. It was always the same, a peanut butter and jelly biscuit thrown into a paper bag. On this particular day the sack had dirt in it, probably potatoes, or onions had been bought in the sack. At lunch I got my usual cup of water and I sat down to eat my lunch. There was so much grit in the peanut butter and jelly biscuit that I could not eat it. Evidently, someone saw me trying to eat that sandwich, which of course I could not eat.

When I got back to class the teacher called me up front, and told me I needed to go to the principal's office. I was scared that I had done something wrong, and was in trouble. But when I reported, he told me from now on every Monday when you get to school, come to my office and I will give you tickets to eat in the lunchroom for that week. I was so embarrassed and ashamed because I knew someone had seen me. I never went back to that school another day in my life. To my knowledge my dad never once asked me why I was not in school. I don't think he cared if I got an education or not, since he only had a third grade education.

Going Through Home Again

The next year we moved to Good Hope, Alabama. My new school was a small, white frame building. I saw boys my age who appeared to be about as poor as I was, so I started back to school on my own, without any encouragement from my dad, or stepmother. I worked in the cotton fields in the fall to get money for clothes, shoes, and school supplies. My dad would take me to an Army surplus store in Cullman, and buy my shoes for a little of nothing. The shoes were much too large for a little boy. I packed paper in the toes in order to keep them on my feet.

LJ at Age 12

Going Through Home Again

I was so nearsighted that I could not read the writing on the chalkboard. This actually started when I first went to elementary school in Cullman. The teacher had me sit on the front seat, but even there I could not see the writing on the chalkboard. They would send notes home to my dad, telling him that I could not see. He would tear them up and throw them in the trash. It was about this time that my dad started bootlegging. I would have to help carry water from the well at night, into the woods, to fill the still.

My sister Betty was four years younger than me. Betty and I picked peas for a local farmer that year. It was getting late in the season. He had to get them out of the fields or they were going to spoil. He told us that if we would pick the peas, we could have half of what we picked. That winter we ate peas, corn bread, and occasionally an opossum. The peas were so full of weevils that you had to let them simmer in the bowl until the weevils floated to the top, then dip them out to eat the peas. I never remember my dad telling me he loved me until I was grown. I remember him telling me quite often how stupid I was.

He would call the names of some of the boys in our neighborhood, and talk about all the things they could do and ask me, *Why do you have to be so stupid?* I grew up believing that there was something wrong with me. I believed I wasn't as smart as other people my age. I felt non-existent. I left home when I was twelve

Going Through Home Again

years old. I went to Cincinnati, and lived with an older sister and her husband, who also happened to be an alcoholic. I was once again surrounded by abuse. I saw him beat my sister in the face, with his fist. I recall a time when he gripped her by the hair of her head, and slammed her face into a bathroom mirror. The mirror broke, and cut her face up pretty bad. When she died at age fifty-five, the scars were still very visible on her face.

However, there were advantages to living with them. I had good food to eat, clothes to wear, and thank God my sister took me to an optometrist who examined my eyes, and fitted me with a pair of glasses. When I walked out of the office onto Vine Street in Cincinnati, I saw things I never even knew existed in the world. It was one of the most amazing moments in my life. I enrolled in Rothenberg Jr. High School. I had completed the seventh grade at Good Hope. Things went well for the first year and then my brother-in-law went back to drinking, and having various affairs.

When Bill would get drunk, my sister Margie would take me out of school in Cincinnati, and take me back to Birmingham, to enroll me in school there. After a few weeks, when he sobered up, he would come to Birmingham, and beg her to come back home. She would take me out of school in Birmingham, and put me back in school in Cincinnati. This was probably the most difficult time of my life. I was a young boy with no self-esteem. As soon as Bill got drunk again,

Going Through Home Again

we went back to Birmingham. This process happened until I was a few days short of finishing the tenth grade. When she took me out of school that time, and back to Birmingham, I determined that I would never experience that again. Another older sister, Jane, and her husband had just purchased a restaurant in Tarrant City, Alabama. Ernie, my brother-in-law, had been a truck driver all of his adult life. He owned three trucks, one of which he drove, while hiring drivers to drive the other two.

    They were leased to Alabama Highway Express. Around the last time I moved back to the Birmingham area, he and my sister, Jane, began operating the restaurant. I asked him if he would give me a job. I told him I was not going back to Cincinnati and I was not going back to school. He hired me, and paid me fifteen dollars a week, plus he let me live with them. I probably worked sixty, or seventy hours a week. The restaurant was directly across the street from the Tarrant City Church of God. About the time I started working there, they began a revival with evangelist Billy Franklin.

    There were a number of young people about my age in the church at that time: Rex Taylor, Wayne Chambers, Caroline Oliver, Katherine Walton, Tom Walton, and others. When revival service would end, they would come into the restaurant for a snack. They began to talk to me, and invited me to attend the current revival. I accepted their invitation, and went to church the next night. I had not been in

Going Through Home Again

many churches in my life and I certainly was never in a church of this type. They were in the altar shouting, praising God, and speaking in a language I had never heard. I asked someone what they were doing. *Were they trying to get someone saved...or something?* I really do not know how I even knew enough to ask such a question. Their response was, *Well, we hope so!* The second night I went back and asked the pastor's son Herman *Hank* Thompson, *If I come back tomorrow night will you go with me to the altar?* He said he would, so the next night I came back. I asked someone how to get saved. They responded, *Oh you will know it when it happens.* They were right about that, but that did not tell me how to get saved.

    I don't believe I heard a word the evangelist said that night. I was just waiting on him to stop talking, so I could go to the altar and get saved. When I went to the altar that July night in 1953, I wore the saints out. I prayed for the better part of two hours. Several times, someone would ask, *Son, don't you believe the Lord has saved you?* Each time I responded, *No, Jesus hasn't saved me.* Someone said, *Maybe it's your cigarettes.* I took them out of my pocket, and threw them on the altar. Later someone asked again, *Son, don't you believe Jesus has saved you?* Again the answer was no. Someone then said, *Maybe it's your ring.* I had a cheap ring on and I took it off and threw it on the altar. If they had said it was my shirt, I would have ripped it off, and threw it on the altar! After about two hours, whether in a vision or not, I truly do not know, but I saw the most beautiful sunrise I had ever seen in my life, and no one had to ask, *Don't you believe Jesus has saved you?* I leapt to my feet shouting, clapping my hands, and praising God. Shortly after my conversion experience, I was baptized in a little creek not far from the church. Later, I received the baptism of the Holy Spirit and I joined all those other shouting, tongue talking Christians. One of the most amazing things about the situation is that my brother-in-law bought the restaurant at that particular time. He only kept it for approximately one year, and then sold out. He went back into the trucking business, and stayed in that business, until he retired. It was a new beginning for me, yes, but it was more than that. I did not realize that it was the first step God had planned for me. A first step that would lead to the restoration of everything darkness had stolen from my family.

Going Through Home Again

Bill & Margie at the House where LJ Grew Up

3
THE CALL OF GOD

When I was seventeen years old, God called me to preach. There are many older people who will remember the lyrics, *I can tell you the time, and I can take you to the place, where the Lord saved me by His wonderful grace.*[3] That is a reality in my life also. In addition to that, I can tell you the time and place, where the Lord called me to preach the glorious Gospel of Jesus Christ.

At that time I was a blank slate as far as the Gospel and Christianity was concerned. I did not even know what the scripture excerpt, John 3:16 was about. No one but God would have called me to do anything significant. Again, in my eyes, I was insignificant. Later in life, I looked back, and realized there were at several times that I should have died, and would have except for the mercy of God. The first time was when I was eight years old.

I came home from my mother's funeral, and had a severe case of colitis, even though at the time I did not know what that was. I only knew that when I went to the outhouse, I could not get back to the main house, before I had to turn around, and go back. My condition continued to deteriorate over the next few days. The doctor instructed my dad to refrain from

---

[3] Pace, Adger M. *Church Hymnal.* Cleveland, Tennessee: Pathway Music, 1979. Print.

Going Through Home Again

giving me food, and to only allow me to drink juices. After a short while, I sank into a coma. The doctor told my dad I was dying. Later dad would tell me, he decided that if I was going to die, I was not going to die hungry. He began to feed me corn bread and milk. I began to recover. During the coma I had what I describe as a *dream vision*. I saw my older sister Margie, and a young boy, named J.C. Stapp, who was a friend.

They were sitting on a quilt out in the front yard, under a walnut tree assembling a B.B. gun for me. I never had any toys to speak of in my life. I usually played with one of mom's pot lids. I sometimes would roll an old tire, play with a homemade rubber gun, or with a slingshot. I was so excited to get that B.B. gun, and while stuck in my delirium began to ask daddy to get me some B.B.'s so I could shoot my B.B. gun. He told me that when I got well, he would get me some B.B.'s. With that blessed encounter I began to struggle to get well. I regained consciousness at some point, but was not strong enough to walk. We lived in a three-room house, with two bedrooms and a kitchen. In each bedroom, there were two double beds.

Believe me when I tell you, I can still remember the first step I took, during recovery. I could only take one step, from one bed, and I would catch myself on the other bed. After a while, I got strong enough to hold on to the foot of the bed, then the wall, and walk to the kitchen table to eat. That was such a wonderful experience; I don't know how to describe it!

Going Through Home Again

After a few days I was out running and playing. The second near death experience happened on a Sunday afternoon. Several of us little boys went to an old lumber mill to play. There was a cable car that was used to pull logs up a steep incline, to the mill from the edge of the wood. A hand crank pulled up the carriage, while a cable was wound up on a heavy metal spool, and when the carriage was released it would run very rapidly to the bottom of the incline. Two, or three of us boys decided to wind it up, and ride back down the hill. When it was pulled back up the hill, I jumped on the front of the carriage, unaware that the cable was looped up, and sticking out in front. When I jumped on the carriage, it started moving very rapidly down the hill. My right leg was caught in the loop and I was almost pulled underneath the carriage. I managed to hang on, but skin was ripped off my shin down to my toes.

I was terrified! At the time I believed what had saved me, was the fact that I was barefooted. I knew shoes would have caught, and pulled me under the car. Today I know better! What saved me was the fact that God had plans for my life. I learned that any person, circumstance, or accident, shall not interrupt His plans. *God is the cupbearer of fate, not humanity.* The third incident occurred, after my mother died. Upon her death, there was a stark change in the household. I was not given a lot of attention. I remember one time when I went to Decatur on the back of a small motorcycle with J.C. Stapp.

Going Through Home Again

He was the same boy I saw helping my sister assemble the B.B. gun for me, under the walnut tree in my vision. The motorcycle quit running in Decatur and J.C. could not get it fixed. We pushed it back to Cullman, approximately thirty-five miles. J.C. was about three years older than me, and he had a paper route in Cullman. He worked out of a small building on the east side of town. It was late when we got back and so I spent the night with him in the newspaper building. I was gone two or three days and my dad never asked where I was, or showed any concern.

It was as if he never knew I had been gone. There was another incident with J.C. where, I could have been killed had it not been for the mercy of God. J.C. Stapp and I walked in the woods from Cullman to the city dam. We walked a long way through the woods. Again, keep in mind that J.C. was a few years older than me, and much larger. When we got to the dam, the water was high going over the dam and cascading violently below.

There were high and low places in the dam. In the low places, water rushed through, and was covered with some sort of slime, or moss that was extremely slippery. The drop was twenty, or twenty five-feet below. I was really scared to cross, because I did not know how to swim. The only reason I followed J.C. was because we had walked so far through the woods and I did not know how to find my way back home. J.C. would not turn back, though I begged

Going Through Home Again

him to. I was a skinny, frail little boy with small feet. If my feet would have slipped, there is no doubt I would have drowned that day. Again, God was with me, because He had a purpose for my life. I had no knowledge of what an exciting journey lay before me. When I became a Christian, and began attending church regularly, I remember hearing the pastor say, *Sunday is the Lord's day and we are not supposed to work on Sunday. We are to attend worship.* I went to my brother-in-law, who had so graciously hired me, and told him I could not work Sundays anymore, because the preacher told us we were supposed to go to church. My brother-in-law told me, *If you can't work on Sundays, I can't use you, because that is the day I need you most.* Without one thought about what would happen to me, I decided to quit. The next day I went up the road to an A&P grocery store, and asked the manager if he needed any help. Lo and behold, he hired me on the spot. I went to work for forty dollars a week. To earn that much money, I had to work forty-eight hours a week.

After tax deductions I drew about thirty-five dollars a week. A few weeks later I heard the pastor say something about tithes. I asked one of the boys after church what it meant to tithe. He explained that when God blesses us with an income, we are told in the Bible that we should return a tenth of it to the Lord. We do this, he said, by giving to the church to support the work of God. The next week I got a tithe envelope, and started paying tithes. As I write this story, I am nearly seventy-eight years old and I still pay my tithe. I could not even fathom that the small amount I was giving to God would be repaid, and multiplied in so many different, amazing ways over the course of my life.

Lonnie Gable Sr. & Ethel (top)
LJ Gable & Perny Williams (bottom)

4
THE PREACHING BEGINS

I was so happy after my salvation experience that I wanted to tell everyone. I wore my fellow employees out telling them about Jesus. I would tell them, *You need to go down to that little, cement block church, Jesus saved me and I believe He will save you.* In that small, cement block building there was no air conditioning, so we used funeral home fans. There were no screens on the windows.

In the summer the choice was to keep the windows closed, and fan, or open the windows, and fight the bugs. The building was heated in the winter with some sort of a stove sitting out in the floor. To me it was the grandest building on earth. After a while the other employees starting trying to avoid me, because they knew I was going to tell them they needed to get saved. This went on for a while, but they couldn't escape. I would look them up, and tell them about Jesus! So they began to question me about what that little church believed in.

I explained it to them in a clear as mud fashion, *They don't believe in drinking, they don't believe in smoking, going to movies, or women and men swimming together. They don't believe in going to ball games, picture shows, or dances. They don't believe in women wearing britches, make-up, jewelry, or cutting their hair.* I had it down to a science, but one day it dawned on me, that I did not know one thing they *did* believe in.

Going Through Home Again

There were two things I did know. I knew Jesus had come into my life as Lord and Savior, and I knew God had called me to preach. I could not believe it, but some how I knew it was real. How could God call someone like me to preach? I knew squat about the Bible. I was the one who carried

Letha DeBusk

notes to Judge Kenneth Griffin's office, in the Cullman County Courthouse, when my dad was supposed to be there for a hearing. He would be arrested for hauling liquor, and when the hearing date arrived, he would send me with a note telling the court he was sick, and unable to be there. I knew it was all a lie. Until this day, I do not really know what kind of relationship my

Going Through Home Again

dad had with Judge Griffin. We did rent an old shack of a house from the Judge and he always seemed to be concerned for our family. I believed that he took care of us because he knew we were living in poverty. That is probably why my dad made and sold liquor.

After a few weeks of working at the A&P store, I decided to go sit in my car, and eat alone one day at lunch. I did this because the other men would curse, smoke, and tell dirty jokes during the lunch break and I did not want to hear it. Sitting in an old, 1947 Chevrolet car, listening to southern gospel music, and praying at lunch break, God called me to preach. The call of God was imprinted in my mind, soul, and spirit. The moment I was called is a moment that defies explanation. I could not believe what was happening. I talked to the pastor of the church, and told him what had happened.

He put me in a youth program with a small speaking part. Later, he asked me to prepare, and preach a sermon during the Wednesday night meeting called Y.P.E. or, Young People's Endeavor program. That was my first attempt at preaching. The entire message probably did not last six minutes. When I could not think of anything else to say, I just sat down. That was the beginning of a journey that would last more than six decades. By that time my dad had moved to Cincinnati and I visited on a mission to get him saved. I found a church in a little storefront building on Liberty Street that was in revival. I did not know at the time, that it

Going Through Home Again

too was a Church of God, but it turned out that it was. I got my father to go to church with me one night. A number of wonderful things happened. My dad was gloriously saved and I met a young girl (Patricia Mae Hall), who was playing the piano for the worship service. I talked with her briefly and I got her phone number.

When I got back to Alabama, I called her and we talked some more. Shortly after that, I decided to move back to Cincinnati so I could spend time with Patty. Before meeting her, I had been on a few dates that never amounted to anything, but this time it was different. I found Pat to be an outstanding Christian. Not only was she a wonderful Christian, but also she knew how to play the piano, and I had been called to preach. We started going steady, as we called it back then, and I went to see her every night, minus one, over the next several months. I asked her to marry me, and she said yes, but I had to get a yes from her mother also.

Pat's dad, Silas Hall, had been killed in a coal mine explosion near Beckley, West Virginia, when Pat was nine months old. She had an older sister Juanita, and a brother, Cleadith. When Pat was six years old, her mother met a man, Charles DeBusk from Covington, Kentucky. They were married, and he moved the family to Covington. That is where they were living when I met her. When I asked Pat's mother if I could marry her daughter, she wasn't very happy about that, because we were both only seventeen. After some time she consented. She still did not appear

Going Through Home Again

to be very happy about it and everyone was certain that the marriage would fail because we were so young. We were both eighteen when we married in her mother's living room, December 12th, 1954. At the time of this writing we have been married fifty-nine years. I tell everyone that I speak with; the best thing that ever happened to me was when I became a Christian, followed by when I married Patricia Mae Hall. I am so happy to report that after my dad's conversion experience, he served the Lord faithfully the rest of his life. He was in his mid-fifties when he accepted the Lord Jesus as his Savior.

He became active in church, later serving as Sunday School Superintendent for a few years. He died two weeks before his seventieth birthday. The only comment he made to me after his salvation experience was this, *I don't know if I can quit smoking or not. I have been smoking since I was twenty-one years old.* Of course, I was just a boy, and a new Christian myself. I really did not know what to say so I simply replied, *Well dad just pray and ask God to help you.*

To my knowledge, he never smoked another cigarette as long as he lived. I have made some alarming statements about my dad, but in all fairness to him, I want to add more commentary. As I mentioned, he only had a third grade education. He dropped out of school to work on the farm, and help provide for the family. The only thing he knew about rearing children was what he had learned from observing his parents. It is my understanding

Going Through Home Again

that his father was abusive to him, and his siblings. Grandpa Gable died when my dad was twelve years old. At the age of fifteen, dad went to work for a veterinarian, Dr. Steward, in Cullman. He worked for him for twenty-one years. Dr. Steward finally let him go, because of his drinking problem. By that time he had become a good veterinarian in his own right, but he was not licensed to practice. There is a possibility he could have been grandfathered in, but I am sure he did not know about those things, and of course those things may not have been in play in 1936. He did continue doing that type of work on his own, until the law began to enforce the license requirements. After that my dad did hard manual labor. There were times when he walked seven miles to work, unless someone would stop, and give him a ride.

When he got off work he had to walk home, or hitch a ride. His feet were in terrible shape with corns and bunions. When he got home he was hobbling along, barely able to walk. I saw him come in with water sloshing in his shoes, where he had sweated so much during the day. As if those problems were not severe enough, by the time he was forty-seven years of age he had buried his wife, Ethel and three children. I mention these things so no one will think I have anger or bitterness toward my dad. He wasn't living a Christian life at that time. Life was hard, and with very little education he simply did the best he knew how to do. When I became a Christian in 1953, I knew nothing

Going Through Home Again

about God, religion, the Bible, or church. There was not one person in my family saved that I knew of. I did have one aunt, Cora Green, who talked about going to church. She seldom ever went, because she had no way to get to church except to walk. When she did go, she went to the Church of Christ. I do know that she listened to preaching on the radio. Her husband, Uncle Roll, would curse them while she was listening. He most often referred to preachers as old money beggars. I had three uncles who went to prison for murder. Two of them went for multiple murders. My mother's brother, Dock Freeman, killed Homer Boyd, and was sentenced to life in prison, but was released after fifteen years. After his release he came to visit us in Cullman.

Going Through Home Again

    I had heard my dad say, *I just don't believe that Dock killed Homer.* A few years later Dock killed another man, his nephew, Sammy D. Freeman. Ironically, Sammy's father had also been murdered, when he was twenty-six years old. When Sammy's dad was murdered, he had two children, and his wife was pregnant at that time with Sammy. In the same tragic fashion, Sammy was twenty-eight years old, had three children, and his wife was pregnant when Dock killed him. Uncle Dock went back to prison, and he stayed until old age. When they released him, they would not allow him in Cullman County. However, when his mother, Margaret Freeman died, my sister Margie smuggled him into Cullman County for the viewing.
    My uncle, Donald, who was really my great uncle, and fairly wealthy, or at least I thought so, killed two men in Georgia. He did not go to prison for that. He owned a good size farm and a grocery store, in Bug Tussle. He had several people who worked for him. Uncle Donald always drove a big, red and black, international truck and he carried a lot of money in his pocket. He was drunk every time I ever saw him. He sat on our back porch, and talked with my dad, when I was just a small boy. He was drunk as always. He sat there until he collapsed, and I remember my dad, alongside another man, loading him in his truck, then taking him to the hospital. His bladder had ruptured (his prostate they later said, was swollen, too large to pass urine). He did not die and he continued drinking.

Going Through Home Again

  Later on down the road, Donald went out to party with a friend, and another uncle, Alphonse. They knew Donald always carried a lot of cash, and they wanted it. Donald got so drunk and he passed out. Alphonse, and his partner in crime, drove Uncle Donald out into the country. They drove his truck up on a steep slope, placed Donald on the road, put his upper torso doubled over his legs, then pushed the truck over on him. He died instantly. Alphonse and the other man were arrested, tried, and sentenced to prison. A few years later Alphonse was murdered in prison.

  Even unto this day I have family members in prison for serious crimes. My cousin, Charlie Seiler, had a son named Todd who died from an overdose a few months ago. Charlie's older brother is in a mental hospital in Birmingham because his brain has been destroyed by drug use. The list could go on and on, but the evidence is clear. I am not proud about these things, yet I am grateful that the Lord delivered me out of the generational curse.

  Pat and I were married almost two years, when God blessed our union with a beautiful little baby girl. She weighed in at seven pounds, eight ounces. When Teresa was one month old, we almost lost her to death. She developed Pneumonia in both lungs, and for a while we did not know if she would live, but God graciously heard our prayers and He spared her life. We attended the 4th Street Church of God, where Pastor James Chamberlain served.

Going Through Home Again

He and his wonderful wife Betty showed us kindness. They tried to help me in my ministry. Pat's mother, Mrs. Letha DeBusk, had started the church in a store building after conferring with A.M. Phillips, State Overseer of Kentucky. She had been taking Pat to church in Cincinnati, but they had to ride a city bus and the commute was long.

In the winter months it was very difficult for them. At the annual church convention in Lexington she met with Overseer Phillips, and asked what they needed to do to get a church in Covington. He explained she would need to get a building; to get chairs and furniture. Additionally, she would need thirty individuals to sign up that they wanted a church, and that they would support a minister. She did just that and Bishop Phillips appointed John Gilliland of South Carolina to pastor the New Mission Church.

I was restless, and moved our little family back to Birmingham for about one year. I worked for Hayes Aircraft in Birmingham for approximately one year, got laid off, moved back to Covington, and went to work for American Standard Plumbing & Heating Company in Cincinnati. Pastor Chamberlain had purchased property on 4th Street in Covington to build a new church. They were worshipping in a tent, on a lot next to the building site. We reconnected with the Covington church. After a while, always restless, and trying to find my way, we moved our membership to Crescent Springs, where E.C.

Going Through Home Again

Campbell was serving as pastor. We became very active in the Crescent Springs Church of God. Our pastor, Reverend E.C. Campbell, was the kindest man I had ever met. After a while he asked me to teach the teenage Sunday School Class. I agreed and I became the teacher even though I still severely lacked knowledge of the Bible. This was probably one of the best things that could have happened to me. We had approximately twelve to fifteen students.

This was a wonderful opportunity for me because I began to study the Bible and the Sunday school lessons. Up until that time I really did not know much about the Word of God. There came a time when I became discouraged and wanted to quit, but Pastor Campbell encouraged me to keep on teaching, and I did. He became the most influential mentor of my life. Meanwhile, we were attending Crescent Springs when our first son, Gary Wayne, was born, April 18th, 1961. Gary weighed in at eight pounds and he was a welcome addition to our family. Mrs. DeBusk had four granddaughters at that time, but no grandsons.

You can understand why he was so special. Perhaps the greatest thing Pastor Campbell did was to get me involved in working as a boys counselor at summer youth camp. The camp was held at Levi Jackson Park in London, Kentucky. It was a beautiful setting out in the woods; we slept on bunk beds in cabins, while eating together in the cafeteria and we could swim in the park pool.

Going Through Home Again

At night we had revival, camp meeting style services in the cafeteria. Pat and I began working camp, when the children were old enough to take along with us. This continued for a number of years. She served as head counselor for the girls, and I for the boys. One summer, the evangelist was the State Youth & Christian Director of Georgia. It was in one of those services that God really got a hold of my heart and reminded me, He had called me to preach His gospel. He did not call me to quit!

I went back home with a new determination to continue serving the Lord, however, I was still struggling and could not understand why. The great thing is, I had a wonderful, Godly wife who knew how to pray. She would pray until, as she would say... *I prayed through.* God helped me to get a better understanding for the Word and my relationship with Him. Today I understand I was trying to go to Heaven, because of my righteousness. One day I read in Isaiah 64:6 (NKJV), *All of our righteousness is as filthy rags.* The real turning point came when I read Jeremiah, 31:31-34 (NKJV),

> ***31*** *Behold, the days are coming, says the* L*ORD,* *when I will make a new covenant with the house of Israel and with the house of Judah—* ***32*** *not according to the covenant that I made with their fathers in the day that I took them by the hand to lead them out of the land of Egypt, My covenant which they broke, though I was a*

Going Through Home Again

*husband to them, says the L*ORD*. **33** But this is the covenant that I will make with the house of Israel after those days, says the L*ORD*: I will put My law in their minds, and write it on their hearts; and I will be their God, and they shall be My people. **34** No more shall every man teach his neighbor, and every man his brother, saying, 'Know the L*ORD*,' for they all shall know Me, from the least of them to the greatest of them, says the L*ORD*. For I will forgive their iniquity, and their sin I will remember no more.*[4]

What a joy to finally realize that Jesus had purchased my salvation on Calvary. To know that it wasn't about me, and what I had done, or what I was doing. It was about Jesus, who He is, and what He had done for me. The joy of the Lord came back into my heart and I wanted more than ever to serve Him. I was in my mid-twenties, when I first began to realize that God was calling me to be a pastor. I talked with Pastor Campbell and told him how I felt.

He said he would help me if that was what I believed God was calling me to do. Later he talked to the state Overseer of Kentucky, Bishop Earl Palk, and there was talk about appointing me to a small church in Kentucky. However, God had other plans for my life. I had a wife and two children to support. A small church would probably not be able to take care of us.

---

[4] *The Holy Bible: Containing the Old and New Testaments: NKJV, New King James Version.* Nashville, TN: Nelson Bibles, 1982. Print.

Going Through Home Again

    Also, there were not any jobs available for me in that small town. God began to deal with me to go to Dayton, Kentucky, and plant a new church. Again I went to Pastor Campbell, and told him how I felt. He agreed to help me get a church started in that small town, on the banks of the Ohio River. I found a building that had been flooded by the Ohio River a couple of years earlier. It had been a small grocery store. The front windows were boarded up. The floors inside were three inches deep in dried mud. The plumbing was rotted out, and it looked almost impossible to fix. I talked to the lady who owned the building and she told me that if I wanted to fix the building up, she would give me free rent in exchange for materials, as well as my labor.

    The rent would be thirty-five dollars a month, after I had been reimbursed for materials and labor. I hauled the dried mud out of the building, remodeled, put in new water lines, and painted inside and out. I built a Bible stand out of a floor model television cabinet. I took all the insides out, covered the outside with knotty pine paneling, and put a laminate top on it. I purchased some wooden theatre chairs that were connected in sections of four. I painted the bottom half of the chairs black and the top half gold. About that time I learned of a hotel over in Cincinnati that was remodeling, and had a lot of carpet they were replacing. I went to ask if they would give the old carpet to a small church. They said, *The carpet is yours; all you have to do is haul it away.*

Going Through Home Again

First church pastor Gable pastored, Dayton, Kentucky July 4, 1970.

5
BUILDING THE TEMPLE

There was enough carpet to cover the floors, walls, ceiling, and roof of the church. I took it to the church, where I was a member. Pastor Campbell showed me how to cut out the very best parts of the carpet, turn it upside down, and stitch it together. When it was finished, it was absolutely beautiful. There is no doubt it was very expensive material, and it looked as if it had never been stepped on. After that I built an altar out of two by four lumber, and covered it with a scarlet colored material. Everyone who came into the little church was amazed at how beautiful it was.

The work was done in May of 1965. I turned my attention to gathering a congregation. Back in those years it was uncommon for the Church Offices, or other local churches to send members, or money to help plant a new church. I walked the streets of Dayton, Kentucky, visiting every house that would allow me to visit. I passed out tracts and leaflets telling everyone who would listen that I was starting a Church of God on 4th street in Dayton. I concluded my visitation work after two weeks and I finalized my opening plans. The population of Dayton, Kentucky was 97% Catholic; the other 3% was a mixture of several different denominations. There were a few Church of God people in Dayton, but they drove to other churches in Newport or Covington. The first service we had

Going Through Home Again

in the church was on July 4th, 1965. There were no members sent from any other Church of God congregation to help us. My mother-in-law went with us for support, as well as, Ralph and Neva Campbell.

    The Campbell's came to us from the Assembly of God in Bellevue, Kentucky. That was all the help we had. The very first Sunday, we had forty-three in Sunday school and worship service. Seven months later, we set a record with one hundred-fifty seven in Sunday school and church. We had a small sanctuary and we had two small classrooms in the back. On that Sunday morning, the adult teacher moved all the chairs out of the classroom, except one. Everyone stood up for class, while the teacher stood on the only chair, in the corner of the room. No one was more shocked than myself. It was then that God

Going Through Home Again

reminded me, that this was not my doing, but His. While building the church, I was working a full-time job to provide for my family because the church wasn't able to pay me. I have stated on many occasions, that I paid the church to let me be their pastor and I didn't mind doing that except, they acted like I was getting the best end of the deal! When the church began to average approximately one hundred in worship, I realized that if we continued to grow, or even hold on to the ones we had, we needed to build a church. We had no money, most of the people were poor, and I wasn't sure what we could do. So we did what we could do, we prayed!

About that time, a nice brick home in Dayton with some acreage went up for sale. I met with the older couple that owned the property. They told me the asking price, and it was out of reach for our small congregation. I explained the situation to the State Overseer. He suggested I offer them considerably less than they were asking. Even at that lowered amount I didn't know how we could buy the property. We were buying our home in Erlanger, and decided to sell our house for equity on a down payment, if the couple would agree to the price. When we talked with them they explained, there was no way they could possibly sell for that price. We left their home very sad and unsure of what to do next. Again, I did what I could do, I prayed. Several days passed then the man called me and he wanted us to meet with him again. We met at the appointed time and he began to explain.

43

Going Through Home Again

He and his wife could not sleep, so they got up at two in the morning, and went for a walk. He told us that God spoke to him. God told him that He wanted us to have the property. He talked it over with his wife and they agreed to sell it to us at the price we had offered. God had answered our prayers! We purchased the property. Pat and I sold our home in Erlanger, and used the equity we had in it to pay down on the church property. Later the State Overseer would ask me if I had made arrangements to get our money back when the church was able to repay it. I responded, *I was so excited to get the property I never even thought about the money!* We moved into the new parsonage. The problem was the church was still broke, so Pat and I paid the payments out of my earnings. We built a beautiful new church on the property then moved into it. In the later part of 1967, the church began to pay the payments on the new property. Pat and I continued to pay the parsonage payments, until I realized I would not be pastor there forever.

I quit my job, asked the church to support my family, and to pay the parsonage payments. I told Pat that I wanted to prepare the people. It would not be right for another pastor to come in and the membership expect him to pay the parsonage payment. May 21st, 1968, there was another highlight of our life. God blessed us with the birth of our third child. Michael Ray arrived at eight pounds, eight ounces. This brought us great joy, but trouble was on the horizon.

6
THE TESTING OF OUR FAITH

Gary, Pat, Mike, LJ, and Teresa (left to right)

Shortly before we purchased the property, and built the church there was a man; Gary Wittenberg, his wife and two children who attended services. They had been excommunicated from the Church of God of Prophecy. He showed me a letter they had written to him. In the letter they informed him, that they were continuing to pray for his

Going Through Home Again

salvation. They brought into our church a large number of relatives. They were very soon contributing more money into the church than all the other members combined. Shortly after they were all there, Gary began to come to me with complaints about other members. One lady was putting color on her hair, while another was wearing a ring. Back in those days, many of the preachers preached against everything. I knew of nothing wrong with a lady trying to make her hair look nice, or wearing a ring. I refused to get involved in such matters, and as a result, they turned on me.

This fringe group soon began to have secret prayer meetings in their homes. As often happens in these situations, the Holy Spirit supposedly began to speak, and called them out of the church. I had never dealt with anything like this. I didn't even know that Christian people would behave in such a manner. Other than the large Wittenberg family, only two couples left the church.

However, before the actual break, I went through torment, not knowing what to do. There was one night I walked the floor all night long, tormented in my spirit as this was my first experience at pastoral conflict. I was sick with fear and anxiety. Somewhere around two in the morning, I fell on my face before God and poured out my heart. I told God, *This is your church and I have done all I know to do. I want you to do with it whatever you want to do. I don't care if you blow it into ten million pieces. Do whatever you want to*

Going Through Home Again

with it! I can't do any more! I learned a great lesson that night. I learned that God, at times, allows us come to the end of our rope before He steps in. I read in Job 5:8 (KJV), *I would seek unto God, and unto God would I commit my cause.*[5] I overheard one of our church officials quoting this verse out of his own translation. It read something like this, *If I could get to where God is, I would give him a piece of my mind. If that's the way you feel about your problem, just tell God. God ain't fragile. You're not going to break him. He can take it.* When I turned it over to God, He fixed it! He didn't fix it the way I thought He would, or the way I wanted Him to.

    All those people left the church and they took over half the finances with them. Six months later we were breaking tithe records. The attendance continued to grow and we never looked back. It was during my tenure at the Dayton Church that I was elected to the State Youth & Christian Education Board. I am sure this was because I had been so involved in Youth Camp a number of years before I became a pastor. I was already well known by the other ministers in Kentucky. I would be re-elected two years later to serve another term. Throughout the years of my ministry, I would serve four years on the State Youth Board, twenty-four years on the State Council, and six years on the General Benevolence Board.

---

[5] *The King James Study Bible: King James Version.* Nashville: Thomas Nelson, 1995. Print.

Going Through Home Again

The Executive Committee of the Church of God appointed the General Benevolence board position. Fellow ministers elected State Youth & Christian and State Council members. Approximately forty years after I left Dayton, Pat and I were going to Xenia, Ohio, to visit her sister. I told her I would like to go to Dayton, and be in church on Sunday morning. We did and there was almost no one there who recognized us. At the end of the Sunday school class, I introduced myself to the pastor. The pastor was a lady named Joyce Charles. I told her how Pat and I had started the church July 4th, 1965. She invited me to preach that Sunday morning, but I declined. I told her we only wanted to visit, to see how the church was going.

At the end of the service Pastor Charles said to the congregation, *I want to do something for Brother Gable.* She asked all the families who had been saved, then added to the church in recent years to stand. There were twelve, maybe fifteen families that stood. Husbands and wives, along with children and teenagers stood up. Pastor Charles said, *Brother Gable, I wanted you and your wife to see these families. These men and some of the ladies have been saved out of drugs and alcohol, off the streets here in Dayton. Them, and their children, are now active in reaching others for the Lord.* As we were driving on toward Xenia that afternoon, I told Pat, *This is one of the happiest days of my life.*

7
A NEW CULTURE & EXPERIENCE

When we left Dayton, we moved to Hazard, Kentucky, where I oversaw the Maple Street Church of God. We arrived with a U-Haul trailer, and three children, one less than two years old. There was a big snow on the ground, the water was froze up, and not one member came to meet us. With the water froze up there was a problem. We had no milk for baby Michael. I drove to the only store we found open in the little town, which was a bar. Pat went in and she asked the barkeep if he had any milk she could buy. To her surprise, he did. The parsonage was an apartment connected to the back of the church. The heating system was a gas furnace under the floor, with a grate flat on the floor inside the house, and the surface was very hot.

I told Pat, I would have to go to the hardware store, and buy something to put around it, or Mike would get burned. Before I could get out of the house, he fell face forward and burned both hands really bad. Three days after we arrived, someone from the church stopped by to see if we were ok. If ever anyone faced a cultural shock, we did! Pat was born in the mountains of West Virginia, but left when she was six years old. I had never been to the mountains, so it truly was a shock to me. In spite of it all, I was excited to be pastor of the church. The first Sunday we had about fifty in attendance, as everyone came out to see the new preacher. That morning as the congregation was leaving the church, I stood at the front door, shaking hands and trying to get to know as many of the members as possible. The first lady that I shook hands with said to me, *My name is Joan Dieter. I am the only one of the Dieters they have not been able to run off from this church.* Welcome to the wonderful world of pastoral ministry! The church was averaging about thirty-five in Sunday morning attendance, while the tithe approximately was three hundred-fifty dollars per month.

    The building had been in a flood, as it was situated on the North Fork of the Kentucky River. The wooden window seals were rotting so that when it snowed, the snow would blow in on those sitting in classrooms. When I began to talk with the men about remodeling the building, they quickly resisted. They told me how a former pastor had convinced them to build the parsonage on the back of the church. As soon as the project was complete, and they were in debt, the pastor resigned. The church clerk, E.C. Dixon, explained to me that he and his family cooked and sold chicken dinners for several years to pay the payments.

Going Through Home Again

HAZArd - Before

    They were not about to let anyone get them in debt again. Someone told me that the clerk did not care a lot about me being the pastor. Whether this was true or not, I did not know. My first reaction was to get angry. However, I thought about it a while then considered I could hardly blame him. I knew almost nothing about preaching, or being a pastor. Instead the Lord put it in my heart to return good for bad. That very year when Christmas time approached I met with a number of the churchmen.

Going Through Home Again

    I asked them, *What do you do to honor your church clerk at Christmas?* They responded, *We never do anything!* I replied, *Why? This man has been church clerk for almost thirty years. He gets no compensation. You should at least honor him at Christmas*, and they agreed. That year we bought Brother Dixon a nice gift; prepared a surprise party to honor him; I presented a beautiful plaque in his honor; pictures were made of the event, and published in the Kentucky State News. From that time forward I was well thought of by Mr. Dixon. In fact, he became one of the best friends I ever had! God begin to bless, and as so often happens, the devil began to stir up trouble. Some very serious allegations were being made against the ministry and me.

Going Through Home Again

No one wanted to talk to me about it, but Brother Dixon made me aware of some things being said by another minister. He advised me, *You need to go to the State Overseer and talk to him.* I immediately made an appointment with the State Overseer, and went to Lexington to see Bishop McSwain.

When I explained what was happening, he picked up the phone, and called the minister in question. After listening to him for a few minutes the Bishop said to him, *If you have proof that Lonnie Gable has done anything wrong, I want you to bring it and put it on my desk. If you have no proof, I had better not hear another word about it.* E.C. Dixon, and his family proved to be some of the best friends, and some of the best people I ever ministered to during my forty years of being a pastor. I learned several great lessons through all of this. First, I learned that a pastor does not have to do anything wrong to have someone accuse him. The word of God is clear; the devil is the accuser of the brethren! Second, I learned that most people generally respond in kind to how they are treated.

Love them and they will love you back. Treat them with respect and they will treat you with respect. No doubt, there are exceptions to this rule, but in general most people will respond to kindness. In fact, I have often said, the only qualification I felt that I had to pastor a church was the fact that I loved everyone. The power of love is illustrated in the following story:

Going Through Home Again

Hugo Black was a U.S. Senator from Alabama during the late 1920s and early 1930s. When Franklin D. Roosevelt became President, he appointed Mr. Black as an Associate Justice to the Supreme Court. Mr. Black, of course was an attorney, but he never lost his identity as a simple country boy from Alabama. He traveled across the country speaking on different occasions, and always telling little down home kind of stories. One of my favorites was that of the rich landowner, and the poor sharecropper. The story has it that the rich landowner was as honest as the day is long, straight as an arrow, but he was mean spirited, hateful, arrogant, and no one liked him. The poor sharecropper on the other hand was a likeable, warm, and friendly man who just seemed to draw people to him. Everyone loved him, but they all knew he would steal anything that wasn't tied down. He was a thief! The story has it, that he stole a mule from the rich landowner, and someone saw him. He proceeded to notify the landowner, who in turn called the police, and had the poor sharecropper arrested. There was a trial, and the sharecropper asked and received a jury trial. Everyone in the little town there in Alabama knew everyone else. At the trial the evidence was clear, the witness testified, 'Yes I saw him steal the man's mule!' The judge sent the jury back into a little room with the instructions that when you reach a verdict come back out and report. A few minutes later they returned. The judge asked, 'Has the jury reached a verdict?' The jury foreman responded. 'We have your honor.' He

Going Through Home Again

handed the envelope to the judge. He opened and read, 'We, the jury, find the defendant, not guilty providing he will return the mule.' The judge responded, 'That is the stupidest thing I have ever heard of, either he is guilty or he is not guilty. Now you get back into that room and don't come out until you reach a verdict.' The jury shuffled back into the little room and a few minutes later they returned to the courtroom. The judge again asked, 'Has the jury reached a verdict?' The jury foreman responded, 'We have your honor,' and he handed the judge the envelope. The judge opened the envelope and read. 'We the jury find the defendant not guilty, and he can keep the mule!'[6]

That simple little story may sound silly to most people, but I learned a great lesson from it. I learned early on in life, that if we love people, and treat them with kindness, there is almost no limit to what they will do help you. This set the pattern for my ministry throughout life, and because of this I am able to continue successfully in God's calling. During my tenure in Hazard, we not only completely remodeled the church, but we also built an addition to the church. In spite of the blessings that came, I became so depressed that once again, I wanted to quit the ministry. I sat in the nursery for three days and I did not eat. I am not even sure if I prayed. I just sat there in the floor.

---

[6] Newman, Roger K. *Hugo Black: A Biography*. New York: Fordham UP, 1997. Print.

Going Through Home Again

When I got up, I went to Birmingham where I got a job. The owner of a large firm offered me a position where my brother-in-law worked. I agreed to the salary, and the starting date. I went back home with every intention of resigning the church, and moving to Birmingham.

Teresa & Jim at Hazard

When I walked into the parsonage, which was still an apartment in the back of the church, my wife Pat was in the back bedroom on her face. She was praying, crying, and calling my name to God in prayer. I felt like a sheep-killing dog. I waited two, or maybe three days before I called the gentleman in Birmingham, and told him, I just could not leave the ministry. He was very kind, and seemed pleased that I made that decision. We stayed at Maple Street five years and when we left the church attendance was averaging between one hundred-fifty to two hundred people. The monthly tithe was about twenty-five hundred dollars a month.

    I did not know for a long time that two of my predecessors had experienced nervous breakdowns. One of them spent three months in a mental hospital. When he was released, he went back to the church to resign. He then moved to West Monroe, Louisiana, where he served for over thirty years before retiring. One man was reported to have committed suicide in the parsonage. In spite of all these things, I found the people of Appalachia to be wonderful. Hazard is, after all, the town where our daughter Teresa met her future husband, so we really had no choice.

8
BIG CITIES & BRIGHT LIGHTS

In November 1974, we moved to the Pleasure Ridge church in Louisville, Kentucky. This was the first church where I actually was paid a full salary with benefits. They furnished a very nice parsonage on Jamaica Drive, just a few blocks from the church. I was the third pastor the church ever had. Tom Coomer started the church about fifteen years earlier, and served twelve years. Pastor Coomer, and his family sacrificed greatly to the plant the church in Louisville. His dear wife, Sister Pearl, won a drawing at the store where she purchased groceries.

The prize was one thousand dollars. That was in the early sixties when a dollar was worth a dollar. She did not just pay tithes on her winnings, she gave it all to the church! Harden Mushegan followed pastor Coomer. Pastor Mushegan served three years, and moved to California. During my first week as pastor, I was in the church early in the evening of my first week. I was preparing for the Sunday services, when the phone rang. It was pastor Mushegan calling from California. He prayed for me that evening then spoke prophetic words into my life about my ministry. If the Appalachian mountains were a cultural shock, the big city of Louisville was a nightmare of a different color. The area where we lived, Pleasure Ridge, was a very nice pleasant family setting.

Going Through Home Again

The church was also in a good section of the city. The first time I drove to the downtown area was a different story. Going toward downtown on Seventh Street Road was truly unbelievable. I did not realize our culture had changed so much in the few short years we had been isolated in the mountains. The businesses consisted of strip clubs, topless bars, peep shows, adult bookstores, and distilleries. I had heard about these kinds of businesses in New York, but was totally unaware that this immorality had invaded the south. Because of the environment, the members of this church prayed diligently. While still adjusting to the new environment, our youngest son Michael was stricken with Encephalitis.

One day after doing my visitation rounds, Pat met me at the door. She was visibly terrified. She said something is wrong with Mike. He was vomiting. She had taken him to the restroom, washed him, but he had never moved. He was standing up, eyes wide open, but unresponsive. I set him on the side of the bed, pinched him, and slapped him lightly on the cheeks, yet he never flinched. He stared straight ahead, in an almost trance like state. I gathered the little boy in my arms, placed him in the car, and drove to Saint Mary Elizabeth Hospital. They took him into the emergency room. After a short time the doctor escorted us to a small room then explained, *We believe your son has Encephalitis and we can't keep him here. We do not have an intensive care ward in the pediatric department of our hospital.*

Going Through Home Again

We will have to transfer him to Saint Joseph Hospital downtown. He continued, *If our diagnosis is correct, I need to make you and Mrs. Gable aware, there is a possibility that your son will not live. If he does live, he may be blind, retarded, or crippled.* We were terrified! We followed the ambulance to Saint Joseph Hospital.

As they were unloading Michael from the ambulance, he was having a seizure. They rushed him into the emergency room. An hour or so later, the doctor came out. He told us that Mike did have Encephalitis, and that they would not know what the outcome was until he wakes up. The doctor said, *It will probably be ten to twelve days before he wakes up.* We stood by his bedside praying, crying, and calling upon God. We were in a state of shock! Shortly after midnight Mike suddenly woke up! He was calling out, *Mommy, don't let that man hit me any more. He hit me in my back, and hurt me real bad! Please don't let him hit me any more!* I told Pat someone has touched God in Mike's behalf. I stayed a short while longer, and then decided to go home, freshen up, and change clothes. I told Pat, *When I return, I want you to go home, and get some rest.*

I arrived at the parsonage some time after one in the morning. As I pulled into the drive, a car pulled in right behind me. I wondered who that could be at this hour of the morning. I got out, and saw Henry Young. He said, *Brother Gable, we heard about Michael.* Pat and I were in such a state of shock, I don't believe we had thought to call anyone for prayer.

Going Through Home Again

He continued, *Mary Smith, Sharon Holladay, Sue Likens, and Christine Baker got on the phone to call everyone they could. We prayed until some time after midnight when we felt the victory come. We knew that Mike had been healed.* I believe Mike is alive today because those Godly people knew the value of prayer and supplication. Mike not only lived, but also is extremely intelligent, and so are his children. He never had any of the side effects that the doctors mentioned. We are still praising God for the miracle of Mike's life. Early on in my ministry, I realized I needed an education. I was a tenth grade dropout. At age twenty-one, I had taken the GED, and received a diploma from the State of Alabama. In my late thirties I enrolled in the Community College at Louisville. After a few years, I received an Associate's Degree in Psychology.

    I went from there, to the University of Louisville, and continued my studies part-time a few more years. I was also serving on the State Council, teaching in the Bible institute, and serving as District Overseer in one area of Louisville. The membership had every reason to be unhappy, paying me a full salary, and me involved in so many other things. They never complained, in fact they encouraged me to get an education. It is easy to understand why I love, and respect those precious people so much until this day. Even with all of my extra-curricular activities while at the church in Louisville, we out grew the building we were worshiping in.

Going Through Home Again

  We were able to purchase a very large Baptist church building in Shively. They were building a new church building, and wanted to sell the old one. The men in our church were very talented in construction, electrical, plumbing, and painting. We were able to remodel the church without hiring outside workers, and saved thousands of dollars. We purchased the most beautiful furniture, including pews that had inner springs in the seating. I had never seen, or even knew they made such pews. The church was absolutely beautiful.

  The State Overseer, Bishop Clifford Bridges, had tried to discourage us from purchasing the building, because he could not see what our construction crew could see. When the project was completed we invited the Bishop to be a part of the dedication service and he admitted that it was absolutely beautiful. The attendance continued to grow.

Going Through Home Again

When Pat and I left that church in July 1982, the attendance had grown to three hundred plus. I believe the record would show it was the strongest Church of God in Kentucky. When Bishop Bridges tenure ran out, the new State Administrator, Bishop Delbert Rose, asked me to go to the Loudon Avenue in Lexington, Kentucky. That was the church most of the State Office staff attended, and they were in trouble. He believed that my easygoing personality could fit in, and solve their problem.

I was still young and I thought that the Bishop was right next to God, so I should do what he asked. I went to Lexington, but as we were moving into the parsonage on Russell Cave Road, I told Pat that I did not believe we should be here. We stayed there two and one half years. That was the shortage tenure of my ministry. Even though I felt out of place, God blessed the church. During my tenure we received into the church one hundred-fifty members. We did some remodeling of the church building, and purchased land to construct a new building in the future. In September of 1981, I received a phone call from the State Administrative Bishop of Tennessee.

He informed me, that in prayer, he had felt led of God to call me. He wanted me to pastor the Broadmoor Church in Nashville. I explained to him that I had only been in Lexington a short time and I did not want to get into the practice of moving around too much. He insisted that he felt led of God to call me. I told him I would talk to

Going Through Home Again

my wife and family. We would pray, and let him know. At that time I was a member of the General Benevolence Committee. This was the board that gave oversight to all of our homes that took care of children who were orphans, as well as those where parents were not able to keep them. It happened that we had a meeting coming up the next week in Tennessee and I knew that Bishop McSwain would be there. I told him we would let him know something then. He responded, *I need to know something right away, I have several ministers wanting to go there.* I had no intention of going there, so I suggested that he go ahead, and send someone else, because I really didn't think I would move. He again responded, *No I won't do that, I felt led of God to call you, if you decide sooner let me know.* I did not call.

However, when I went to the Benevolence Board Meeting the next week I told Bishop McSwain that we had prayed, and made a decision. We had decided to let him run my name in Nashville. If the Broadmoor Church would receive us, and the Loudon Avenue congregation would release us gracefully, we would trust it was the will of God. We moved to Nashville, early in January 1985. Broadmoor was a wonderful church with a great history. It was especially known for its great music program, after all, the church was located in Music City, USA. The church had a long history of great pastors and music ministers. Pastors such as Dr. Edward Williams, Bennie Triplet, Marshall Roberson, and

Going Through Home Again

other great pastors had served there. They also had enjoyed the services of some of the greatest music ministers in the Church of God. These included ministers such as, Max Morris, Dr. David Horton, and Steve Mauldin. Steve was minister of music when I arrived. He came from a family of talented musicians. His cousin Walter Mauldin led the Lee Singers at Lee University. His dad, Horace Mauldin, had been the music minister in the great Tremont Avenue church in South Carolina for many years. Steve now teaches music at Belmont University, in Nashville.

Kids Kwoir

Going Through Home Again

    With such a great history, and with so many very well educated members, I wondered how a *cotton picker* from Alabama could manage such a congregation. Jeff Conn was finishing up his doctoral program at Vanderbilt University; David Roebuck was completing his doctoral program in church history, at the same school. There were others who had already completed various post-graduate degrees. I once asked Jeff Conn what his doctoral focus was? He responded, *My doctorate will be in Neurological Pharmacology*. I responded, *I would have to go to college just to learn how to say that*. It was a pleasant surprise when I realized they accepted me with grace, and tremendous respect. They soon learned that I had an easygoing disposition, and that they could pick at me. I would not be offended. It was like a match made in Heaven. There would be many battles to fight, but God was so very gracious to us. The church grew, and while I was pastor we built an annex onto the church at a cost of eight hundred-fifty thousand dollars.

Going Through Home Again

Pat became manager of the childcare service called *Wondercare,* and did an excellent job for six years. We stayed on at Broadmoor for nine years. It would be the longest tenure of my ministry. I am sure that I made many mistakes, but the majority of the members were with me all the while. Looking back, I have often said, the biggest mistake I made was allowing Steve Mauldin to resign, and leave the church. When he told me he felt led of the Lord to take a position with a large, prominent church across town, I simply did not have the heart to tell him not to go.

First and foremost, he said he felt led of God. I never wanted to get in the way of what God tells someone. Also, I felt that this was a much better opportunity. Steve was one of the greatest staff members I would ever work with throughout the years. However, Steve was also a man of God. I discovered this when tragedy nearly struck our family once more. Pat had gone in for a routine exam, when the doctor discovered disturbing results.

They had found a lump in her breast and it was cancer. Pat was devastated as she had watched her mother, Letha DeBusk, slowly deteriorate from the disease. We knew that several members were praying for Pat, but Steve happened to be in a fast at that time. Steve, along with the church, prayed for Pat on a Sunday morning. Pat still went in for surgery, the following Tuesday. She was prepped, and taken into the operating room.

Going Through Home Again

The surgery was supposed to last four to five hours. However, after about thirty minutes the surgeon came from the back, approached me, and said, *Mr. Gable, I have good news for you. Your wife doesn't have cancer.* I replied, *Praise the Lord!* He responded, *That is right, praise the Lord!* After Steve left, we looked a few months for a replacement, and then hired a young man named Jonathan Parrish that would become a problem. During my seventh year another young man named Art Hall was elected to the church council. Jonathan and Art became close friends.

They decided (among other young people) that the church needed a younger pastor. When Art went on the council it wasn't long until things began to change. One afternoon, near the end of a council meeting, he asked to make a statement. I granted him the opportunity. He said, *Some members of the church have approached me, requesting a pastoral election.* I told him that was their privilege and that I would contact the Overseer about an election date. I called Bishop McCain the next day, and told him what had happened.

He said, *I will be there next Sunday morning to take a vote.* I announced on Wednesday night that the Bishop would be with us the following Sunday to take a vote. It caused uproar in the church. The vote was taken and I received eighty-five percent of the vote to stay as pastor. I had survived an ouster attempt, but I elected on my own, two years later, to make a change. Prior to my change some of the council

Going Through Home Again

members had pushed me to fire the music minister, knowing that he was involved in the ouster attempt. I declined to let him go. I explained that this was his first and only job as a music minister. His work record would be tarnished. When I left in November 1993, I was not gone more than three months until my successor fired the music minister. However, Broadmoor was a special place on a personal level. It was a place where our grandson's Adam and Justin went to Wondercare. A place where our oldest son Gary married his wife Elke. And Broadmoor was a place where we would make lifelong friends like Mike and Virginia Mason. Broadmoor always had something special happening in the arts, ministries, and the shaping of destinies.

9
THE FAMILY IS SEPARATED FOR THE FIRST TIME

The Gable family has always been tight knit. We never had a lot money, but we always rejoiced in the fact that we had each other. My daughter, Teresa, has pushed me for several years to write this story, even though I did not think anyone would be interested. I have already mentioned that I finally decided to do it believing that God would receive glory.

One other motivating factor was when our current church started to bring in quite a large number of children from the trailer park. I saw the hopelessness in the faces of some of those beautiful little boys and girls. It reminded me of my early years and it hit me; *What God has done in my life, He wants to do in the lives of these precious children*. When God called me to preach, I could not believe it. I still find it hard to understand.

There were so many wonderful young ministers, far more advanced than me in every way. In spite of that, I have never doubted that God called me. As aforementioned, while serving as pastor at Broadmoor, our oldest son Gary got married. He was introduced to his wife through a work friend at the post office, named Steve Strange. While stationed in Germany, Steve had met and married a lady named Andrea Seiler of Sulzbach. Andrea's younger sister, Elke came to visit her sister in Nashville.

Going Through Home Again

Steve asked Gary if he would take Elke out, and show her around, so he did. They picked up a translation book to communicate on the date. Gary and Elke spent a good deal of time together, until she had to return to Germany. After she was back in Germany, they would communicate by phone. A short time later Elke told Gary she was going to come back to America. Gary, always the gentleman, told her, *If you are coming back because you think we are going to get married, please don't, because I am never going to get married*! She came back and before it was time for her to return, Gary had proposed. They were married in 1988, and have blessed us with three beautiful granddaughters.

A few years later we decided to move to a different city and church. Mike was still living at home, and single. I met with him one night in his room to inform him, *Mike, your mother and I have decided that you are never going to get married, and leave home, so we are moving out*! He, of course, understood how very much we loved him and that I was only joking about wanting to get away from him...or was I?

We arrived at the Daisy church in November 1993. We would serve there for approximately seven years. I met some of the most wonderful Christians I would ever know at Daisy. Pat and I had a condo reserved in Panama City when I was hired at Daisy. I asked the council if they were comfortable with me taking a week off so soon after arriving.

Going Through Home Again

The council was very kind, and allowed us to take the vacation, which was nice since we had not been on one in several years. By coincidence, two other couples from the Daisy church were on vacation in Destin. They asked us to join them. We met Emmett Pollard, his wife Jackie, as well as, Leonard Jones, and his wife Vauda. We spent the day together, and cherish those memories. It was a good start. At Daisy we would face different challenges and obstacles, but God is always faithful. The church was considered to be a strong Church of God congregation that averaged almost three hundred in attendance.

They had a respectable music program, not comparable to Broadmoor, but very good. They also had a unique way of selecting board members. They were elected for two-year terms, and there were no limitations on how long one could serve. I very soon learned that there were three board members related to one another, and one other who was like family. They had control over almost everything that happened in the church. I would send out our financial reports, and an agenda ten days in advance of our meetings. I began to notice that everyone had already decided how they were going to vote before we discussed it in the meeting. Shortly after, I learned that those three relatives, along with their long time friend, would meet beforehand to decide how matters would go down. We only had seven board members and the other three were automatically out voted

Going Through Home Again

before it started. I set about to change the process. I asked to make their board selection consistent with church by-laws.

Daisy Church of God

Going Through Home Again

We should vote every two years. The person elected could serve two years, and if re-elected serve an additional two years, then have to go off for two years before being eligible for re-election. This would give other members in the church an opportunity to serve. That stirred up a hornet's nest, but God helped me to get it passed, and that changed the dynamics of the church. The church began to grow and continued to grow throughout the seven years I served. We built a 1.25 million dollar ministry center that was reported by the Chattanooga News Paper to be the best facility of that type in Northern Hamilton County.

The church attendance grew to over five hundred, while the membership increased to six hundred ninety-eight. I found it to be amusing a year or so after I left when O.L. Hart, a retired minister, who had been a member there for several years came to me and said, *Pastor when you came I told some of the members, Lonnie Gable will never be able to hold this church together following our previous pastor. I have to confess you never missed a lick; the church never stopped growing.* What can I say? To God be the glory! While at Daisy, Bishop Walter Atkinson, called Pat and I together. He said, *I want you to go to the South Cleveland Church to pastor.* I responded, *Bishop I do not want to go to South Cleveland.* He could not believe that I did not want to go to Cleveland. Most pastors, as I understood it, would give their eyeteeth to go to Cleveland.

Going Through Home Again

I have never been interested in church politics. Some ministers are, and that is between them and God, but I was never involved in those things. A year or so later I did go to Bishop Atkinson, and ask him to let me go the White House, Tennessee, to pastor. The church there averaged about fifteen to twenty in attendance, and worshiped in a small, remodeled tire store.

The total seating capacity was ninety-five, if every seat in the house was filled. They neither provided a parsonage, nor did they provide benefits. The salary was approximately one half of what I was being paid at Daisy. Bishop Atkinson responded, *No you don't want to go to White House, you need to go see a psychiatrist and get your head examined*! I said, *Bishop you are probably right about that, but I believe this is the will of God for my life.*

He promised that he would think about it. I never heard from him over a period of several weeks. I went back to him again, and reiterated my belief. He promised to think about it, but again several weeks passed where I did not hear from him. I told Pat, *I want you to go with me to talk to Bishop Atkinson. He might think we are getting a divorce, but it is worth a try.* We went together that time, and met him at the State Office in Chattanooga. He listened, then turned to Pat and asked, *Sister Gable, What do you think about this*? She responded, *He believes it is the will of God*. With a drawn out sigh, Bishop Atkinson finally said, *I will go to work on it.* A few weeks later we would make another move, another pastoral change. Before we moved, Bishop Atkinson asked me, *What do you need us to do for you?* I responded, *Bishop, I am not asking for anything.* He responded, *I know that you are not asking, I am asking you, what can we do to help you?* I replied, *The only concern I have is that my health insurance is over seven hundred dollars a month, and the church provides no benefits.* Bishop responded, *I will take care of it for you.* Without me asking, the State Office sent Pat and I one thousand dollars a month for one year.

Rich and Gloria Keen owned a health care facility in White House, and they were aware of our loss of income. She asked me, *Pastor, would you consider working part-time as a hospice chaplain?* I responded in the affirmative, and went to work part-time, choosing my own hours for seventeen dollars per hour, plus car mileage. I never cease to be amazed at God's blessings upon me and my family. When we arrived it was quite a drastic change from where we had been, but I never doubted, that I was in the will of God. The first service we were in at White House, we had a total of seventeen persons present. As I had done throughout my pastoral ministry, I just offered myself to do God's bidding. I have never been one to sit idly by, so I went to work. Shortly after becoming pastor of the small congregation, more people began to come in. It wasn't long until I realized the building was not adequate to house the membership for worship.

Going Through Home Again

If the church was to grow, we were going to need to do something for additional room.

Pat, LJ & Teresa

10
ONCE MORE AROUND THE RIVERBEND

We began looking around for land to purchase where we could build a larger facility. We found property not far from the present location with a nice home, and seven acres of land that was affordable. When we began negotiating with the owner, a minister from a different denomination heard about our plans, and went to work to keep us from building. He went to the city fathers, and took as many people as he could gather to fight against us. We went to several hearings at the Billy Hobbs City Building, but the other denomination's presence in White House was overwhelming. I have nothing against this other denomination, or its people, but I have learned over the years they are very prejudiced against almost all other churches.

Their influence in Middle Tennessee is very strong. It is not uncommon to see two of their large churches directly across the street from one another. There is a very prominent university in Nashville, and many of the members are strong in city politics. When the city refused to allow us to build, Bishop Atkinson wanted to send Dennis Watkins, our church attorney, and file a lawsuit against the other denomination for slander. I told the Bishop, I would rather not do that, and it would be a distraction. I thought it would be a black mark against Christianity to have the Church of God involved in a lawsuit against the other church. I simply did not feel comfortable doing that, and chose to keep looking for property. A great deal of prayer followed, then we chose to build on the land where we were located, and connect the new building to the present building. Afterward, we would completely remodel the old building inside and out. The builders worked to blend in the old with the new.

This we did by the help of God. Next, we purchased property across the street, with a three-bedroom brick house that was converted into a youth center. God blessed everything we put our hands to. The church continued to grow and the finances also grew. By this time my salary had increased, the church was paying my

health insurance, utilities on my home, and putting money into my retirement account. God is truly an awesome God! After serving as pastor at White House for five years, and at age sixty-nine, I decided to retire. Bishop Griffis came and took a vote for a replacement pastor. The church voted for my daughter, Teresa Combs, to be the new pastor.

Going Through Home Again

A large number of the members became angry with me saying that I had come there to set it up for her to be pastor. I repeated this statement over and over, *I never dreamed of Teresa being a preacher, much less a pastor.* The message fell largely on deaf ears. It is not easy to pastor a church, and it is even more difficult for a lady to pastor. Research has shown the three most stressful jobs in America are these; President of the United States, president of a large university, and pastor of a church.

I knew from forty years of experience that it was a very difficult thing to pastor a church, and really did not want my children to pastor. When the vote was taken, a large number of members left the church. Almost without exception, they all told me, *We love Teresa. We know she is a good woman, an excellent musician, and a great singer, but we just don't want a woman for a pastor.* There was another significant number who stayed because the Bishop agreed to come back in one year, take another vote, and if they were not satisfied with Pastor Teresa, he would make another change.

Almost to the day he came back the next year, took another vote, and Teresa got the majority vote again. At that time another group left, feeling confident that the church would have to close. The payment on the property at that time was approximately three thousand dollars a month. As of this writing in the spring of 2014, Teresa has been serving as pastor for nine years, and to my knowledge we have never missed a payment. It is not an overstatement to say that this is truly a miracle of God! For these past nine years I have stayed very active in ministry; preaching revivals, doing marriage conferences, and serving as State Coordinator for the Pastoral Facilitators.

Since retiring from ministry in April 2005, we have traveled to almost every state in the southeast. I have also traveled to Germany, France, and Puerto Rico. One of the highlights of my ministry was to preach in Krewinkel, Germany, in the church Herman Lauster built. Pastor Lauster was one of the great missionaries of the Church of God. He and his wife are buried

on a little knoll behind the church, and a section of the old Roman road runs between the church, and the cemetery. Throughout the years of my life I have been blessed to visit twenty-five different countries. This may be the norm for some people, but for a boy who was half grown before he got out of the small town he was born

Going Through Home Again

in, it was exciting. I have attempted to write the story of my ministry to the best of my ability. I humbly pray that no one will ever think, or believe that I have recorded this for my glory. I have always felt unqualified and unworthy to do the work of God. As I have already mentioned, no one but God would have called me to preach. I was the least of the least in ability. The fact that I loved everyone was a characteristic that I attribute to God, who placed His love in my heart.

    Throughout the years of my life I have learned that the most powerful force on earth is love. Paul speaks of this in 2 Timothy 1:7 (KJV), *For God hath not given us the spirit of fear; but of power, and of love, and of a sound mind.*[7] Again, I have found that if you love others, they will love you back. There are rare exceptions, but most people reciprocate in kind. I have written these words in hope that some other young person may read them, and realize that God can work through anyone who will submit to His will. I also wanted to leave some information for my children in hope that they too will be inspired to do the work of God. I enjoyed going through home again, and remembering the years when God first began to work in my life. Perhaps I needed to remember how God got a hold of me, and changed my life forever. Whatever the reason may be, I want to bless others if possible

---

[7] *The King James Study Bible: King James Version.* Nashville: Thomas Nelson, 1995. Print.

Going Through Home Again

even after I am gone on to be with the Lord. God has so wonderfully blessed Pat and myself with three great children, and eleven wonderful grandchildren. They have brought joy unspeakable into our lives, for which we are eternally grateful. *There is only one life; it will soon be past, only what is done for Christ will last.* I praise God for everything that has happened in my life, and ministry. I can not say it often enough; the best thing that ever happened in my life was when the Lord saved me, and the second best thing was when I married Patricia Mae Hall. The Lord of Glory gave her to me and I am eternally grateful. I am also thankful that at nearly seventy-eight years old, I am still able to be very active in ministry. Looking back, I realize there were many things I should have done differently, but God blessed me in spite of my mistakes. *What God has done for me, He will do for anyone, who calls upon Him*!

The Gable Family in the Early 1900's

Going Through Home Again

Archives

TENNESSEE CHURCH DEDICATES CENTER

The Daisy, Tennessee, Church of God recently dedicated a new $1 million Ministry Care Center that will enhance the congregation's outreach to the growing Soddy-Daisy community near Chattanooga.

According to Pastor Lonnie Gable, the building features a regulation-size gymnasium, a walking track, weight room, and other facilities that will be used by church people and open to the public.

The gym area may also be used as a 750-seat auditorium and can be used for sit-down banquet service. An adjoining smaller dining room with beautiful chandeliers provides space for wedding receptions and similar events. The building also has children's church facilities with built-in puppet stages, a conference room, administrative offices, and several classrooms and storage areas.

Meeting and exceeding local building regulations, the facility has an elaborate sprinkler system and fire-proof walls. A new paved parking area surrounding the building provides parking for 55 vehicles.

Pastor Gable credits hardworking and dedicated church members with achieving the outstanding building project, which was labeled by a Chattanooga news reporter as "head and shoulders above any similar church facility in Hamilton County."

Gable became pastor of the Daisy Church in September 1993. In the five and a half years of his pastorate, he has received 210 persons into membership and has witnessed a tithe increase of some $10,000 monthly. Gable also serves as district overseer of the Daisy District and is a member of the Tennessee State Council.

Lonnie and Patricia Gable

The new Ministry Care Center adjoins the existing Daisy Church of God sanctuary by a handsome walkway that ties the two buildings together.

EVANGEL • April 1999

---

[8] "Tennessee Church Dedicates Center." Editorial. *Evangel* Apr. 1999: 21. Print.

Going Through Home Again

This compilation of news is to acquaint our readers with what is happening in the church world. The *Evangel* does not necessarily endorse the activities reported.

COMPILED BY WILMA AMISON

White House Church Dedicates New Sanctuary

WHITE HOUSE, Tenn.—Pastor Lonnie Gable and 144 church members and friends gathered to dedicate and celebrate the completion of their new sanctuary. Begun in 1994 as an outreach ministry of the Hendersonville Church, with the blessings of Pastor Sam Phillips, the White House congregation's growth was exceptionally slow for the first few years.

For a couple of years, beginning in 1998, Lonnie Gable felt God was calling him to leave his church in Daisy, with a membership of nearly 700, to pastor the small, struggling congregation in White House. By 2000, he had convinced then-overseer Reverend Walter P. Atkinson that this was indeed the will of God, and in April of that year he assumed the pastorate.

In the less than four years Pastor Gable and his wife, Pat, have been there, attendance has increased from the 15 present at their first service to an average of 95 in morning worship services, and finances have increased from only $700 in the treasury to an annual income of $167,339 for 2002-2003, with $47,000 in savings.

Bobby G. Scott, Tennessee evangelism and home missions director, organized the church initially, and this past year he returned to dedicate a beautiful new facility. The old sanctuary, connected to the new, is being enlarged to provide extra space needed for additional classes and a fellowship hall.

Says church member Cheryl Dickerson, "Pastor Gable could have retired, but he chose to take a small church and use his years of experience to help a group of committed Christian pioneers expand the kingdom of God."

Daniel Black Honored

CLEVELAND, Tenn.— Dr. Daniel L. Black, ordained bishop in the Church of God and writer of the adult and youth Sunday school curriculum for Pathway Press since 1981, was the recipient of Westmore Church of God's annual H.D. Williams Heritage Award for 2003. The award, commemorating the vision of Dr. and Mrs. H.D. Williams, is given by the local church to individuals who have made outstanding contributions to the ongoing ministry of the church.

Dr. Black has published hundreds of articles; is the author of two Pathway titles, *A Layman's Guide to the Holy Spirit* and *Never a Day Too Much*, a collection of essays on Christian living; and was a contributor to *The Complete Biblical Library*.

Prior to moving to Cleveland, Dr. Black was a successful pastor for 19 years. In spite of his quiet, unassuming personality, he is a man of strong convictions and an effective communicator. A fellow member said of him, "His communication skills are such that when he makes a statement, no one needs to ask, 'What did he mean?'" His in-depth Bible knowledge has benefitted the Westmore Sanctuary Bible Class for 20 years.

Dr. Daniel Black is loved and respected by those who work alongside him. They have come to know him as a caring person with a pastor's heart. Many agree he is one of the church's most unsung assets.

Church of God Member Authors Children's Book

ST. LOUIS, Mo.—Jennifer Whitter Dunkley, a member of

the Church of God Twin Rivers Worship Center, has completed the first of what she intends to be a series of children's books reinforcing Biblical principles. The stories are written in parable form and are accompanied by simple charmingly expressive illustrations. Details and ordering instructions may be obtained by calling toll free 877-421-7323.

---

[9] Amison, Wilma. "White House Church Dedicates New Sanctuary." Editorial. *Evangel* Jan. 2004: 35. Print.

Made in the USA
San Bernardino, CA
04 November 2015